a Landscape for Loss

a Landscape for Loss

—

erin rodoni

Selected as winner of the National Federation of State Poetry Societies
2016 Stevens Manuscript Competition
by Tony Barnstone

NFSPS Press

This publication is the 2016 winner of the National Federation of State Poetry Societies Stevens Poetry Manuscript Competition, an annual competition with a deadline of October 15th. Complete rules and information on the purchase of past publications may be obtained by visiting NFSPS at www.nfsps.com.

NFSPS Press

Cover art, "Ooze II," Acrylic and Mixed Media on Canvas, 36"x48" by Sarah Meyers Brent, 2013, www.sarahartist.com
Author photo by Gina Logan
Cover and interior book design by Diane Kistner
Book set in Adobe Garamond Pro with Bauhaus titling

ISBN 978-0-9909082-3-4

On *A Landscape for Loss* by Erin Rodoni:

The sky is filled with alchemy and the streets with moped centaurs in this sorcerous, punning, occasionally flamboyant book focused on the author's time in Vietnam decades after the war—Saigon turned into "Sigh gone, the sound / of something you never really grasped / leaving you." It is a book that scratches at at the gutter economics of sex work and "the ghost-itch of the war / that goes on where we can't end it." It is a book that like "the War Remnants Museum, formerly the Museum of American War Crimes" is filled with exhibits and atrocities and elegies, but also of the grace that also goes on and doesn't end, and that swells, pregnant, with hope. It is an amazing book, one that shows us how much can still be gained from a landscape of loss.

—Tony Barnstone

Dr. Tony Barnstone, Whittier College, author of 18 books including *Pulp Sonnets, Tongue of War* and *Beast in the Apartment*

Judge's notes on the 2016 winning manuscript of the National Federation of State Poetry Societies Stevens Manuscript Competition

For Leela

"Grief, terror, love, longing—these were intangibles,
but the intangibles had their own mass and specific gravity,
they had tangible weight."

—Tim O'Brien, *The Things They Carried*

Contents

Prayer for Fertile Ground

This earth's too still to lay a body down.
Parched paddock of my girlhood haunts

barnacled to bedrock in some sorcery of sea
and wind that conjures fog to fill my throat

every time I try to keen. Perpetually
damp and still this ceaseless dimming

into drought, this dirt too thirsty to eat
the dead. Where am I to keep them?

In pasture they lie where they have fallen.
Scavengers hollow but leave the sweet-

familiar ache. I don't want another
rawhide monument in my periphery, the ruin

of skull it winnows to. Still the horizon,
where whitecaps meet mist so seamlessly,

insists: *Desolation.* But I've glimpsed the aftermath
of loss is accumulation. Of moments

after. Of places visited
without. To stay is to bury

X under the same cypress
as a childhood pet. To drive too fast

the same winding shoreline, hugged
in the blind-rush of an unrequited

teenage crush. To rev past those stalled
summers, stockpiled in terracotta veins

on sandstone cliffs where the rib-cave
of an ancient whale is still etched

like a psalm on a page that never flips.
This whole place fades, forever on the verge

of ghosting into fog so deadly
slow it just might stop the world

from quaking. I've laid out all my dead
into an SOS. Sick of waiting

for the promised swarm
of days to chew me

loose, into the alchemy
of distance.

Getting There

When to Go

If you can't have another baby
have another city. Trace its streets

on guidebook maps, until they furrow,
fate-stamped as lines on a palm.

Count its porticoes
like toes—Can you love it?

Saigon. A name that wanes before it waxes
a perfectly dilated absence,

the way history narrows on a war
before rounding to explain it

into past. The way a woman narrows
on her pleasure, before rounding to loose the child

that gathers in her. Hush: the city gathers
ghosts of villages, rounded

in its sprawl. Saigon, the sound of letting go
while moving at great speed. *Sigh gone*

sigh gone. Of boulevards flanked
by plane trees, sigh gone. Of long-boats adrift

amid tangles of water hyacinth. Saigon,
of French villas converted to communist blocks.

Of Minh and his poetry, surrounded
by Cartier, Burberry. Saigon, a city undoing

its incense-fine ancestral helix. Saigon,
a city sculpting real estate of swamp

and sky. Here the future is all
above you the way the traffic

is around you and no one
is inside you. Sigh gone, the sound

of something you never really grasped
leaving you.

What to Bring

Sunscreen, thick
as Greek yogurt,
white as the spectrum
of possible light.
Tooth-smooth pills,
the shake of them
like charms inside
those little yellow jars.
Nets and long sleeves,
our lightweight armor
against a featherweight army
of disease. Aerosol spells
to ward off the blackmagic
of mosquitos, tiny harbingers
of deeper night. They rise
from the brackish water
of my mind, catch like spores
on benign breeze. They are
a dark song pressing
the glass, another's plague
trying to get inside
us. The suitcase
of motherhood
is too much, but must
be carried. Each
talisman promising
protection also warns
of what will happen
if it fails. If the halo
of Deet has a crack,
if fevers séance
from her forehead
and Tylenol can't coax
coolness back. The other
side of the world appears
nightmarescape from here,
but in Vietnam it is
already morning.

Getting Around: On Foot

Daughter,   koalaed to my hips,   eyes the crowd like it can't   touch her.

The heat wears me   out, wears me mean-   eyed, stung.   No one

stops   to let us cross   in this city of the young   melded with

their mopeds.   Not the girls   in hiked-up skirts,   not the mothers,

pokerfaced   as surgeons behind   hospital masks.   At ninety percent

humidity   my don't-   fuck-with-us glance   adheres to my skin.

I know how to win,   haven't I   always? To see without   being

seen,   touch everything   only   with my eyes.   My daughter

believes   I'll never   misstep too soon   from

the curb,   but every day I do   and some crowd-borne grace   swerves

to save us.   Oh God,   what a stranger you are.   I visit only   inside

a makeshift faith   on airplanes   and when I cross   this crowd

of moped centaurs.   Each one a minor   deity. We all are,   aren't we?

We pray to each other   don't   touch me. Then   touch me. At night

I seal our room   into an airconditioned safe-   space, amazed

I've been so close   and haven't.

In Context: This Latitude of Air

"They believed in magic and astrological signs. They were
fatalistic. They were poised as acrobats, always moving in the
direction of the net."

—Ward Just, *A Dangerous Friend*

In this latitude of air
inhabited by windows,

    the unborn hover
    like mosquitos.

        That lightly, and yes,
        they want our blood.

If there's a feather-
weight swarm

    of souls pressing
    light's membrane,

        how to time
        one eyelash-fine

wish to tip
the ancient scales

    of night enough
    to dip a star

        into the incubus
        dark of a woman?

If we are ash
flicked from some

    cosmic cigarette
    aren't we always

becoming less
than what we were?

As soon as the first
cell divides we grow

only by breaking.
City, stalagmite

spiked with lime
and lesion, notice

nothing is rising
down to column

earth and sky. For now
the scaffold holds

my human heaviness,
this meat I wield

and whelk. In sleep
I become so

singular, the context of
my existence wavers

in and out like a radio
station at the edge

of what is known.
Though experience says

I'm the one who's sure
to vanish from

an earth, a universe
never fathomed.

At the War Remnants Museum, formerly the Museum of American War Crimes: Unknown Soldier

Ask for my connection. I'll admit, it's tenuous.
Something about a certain silence in a room

meaning gone, long gone. An uncle
who died young before I was born.

Of course he was beautiful, cocky grin,
laughter caught in his lashes. Black and white.

Airforce pilot. Vietnam. I know he fell
but not how far. But I am here

in the same land from which he vanished.
And here in the city where he was cruel

or crazed, or lost. I've grown into a woman
who has killed only by looking

away at the wrong moment,
who says *atone* and sacrifices nothing

but her sleep. Once I rubbed his name
onto white paper from a wall that held

my gaze, gave it to my father
who tucked it wordlessly away. My father

who never knew war, who draft-dodged
long enough to learn the ways his body

would betray him. In high school
a friend once told me he thought I'd die

young because he couldn't picture me adult.
Sometimes I feel myself pale into the past

beside him, my face on the mantle aching
youth from my nowhere. Dead

or alive, we grow away from the faces
we flare. Ask the city

for a stranger. Ask the stranger
for the right. This room full of pictures

of what boys like him did
asks and asks: *Do you think you are*

kind just because you give
away your hands?

Elegy Proving Airplanes Don't Fly on Shared Belief

Today I smashed into a glass door. Nothing in me knew
I couldn't pass straight through. Still the door

collisioned into existence. My bruised nose in the mirror
the proof—Even so, in the darkened cubby above the city

after my daughter is asleep, the air-conditioner silenced,
letting the night speak heat, I lean my forehead on the window,

all ten fingertips. The empty soccer field below. I swear
I feel my forehead, my every fingertip, ease through,

like a soul pulling free of a body. This is how I go back
to the studio apartment facing the sea, but with no view

of sun bleeding like yolk into its cold boil. I can't prove it yet,
still, but I believe it would take just one more morning

to save you. It would take a rising sun, pink as a newborn
god in his bath of brine. But the sun is always busy rising

elsewhere when it matters. The sea an empty tomb. And we can't
muster enough doubt to roll back the wall, to feel the real

of your wounds. We have only this room in which to act.
Adulthood is the sanest gold. It molds in slats of venetian blinds,

still closed at noon. It strangles like a canary in the dank daylight
of extended adolescence. We are still young enough to drug our tribe

immortal. "What is the value of a single life" is the pseudo-
philosophical discussion we are having. *What is the value of mine?*

is the question the boy contemplating dying really asked. *Jesus
was only a man* someone says, missing the point. It's true,

you've accomplished nothing, not yet, but if you had only lounged
a little longer in the sweet-damp of early bodies, the human-meat

of unbrushed teeth, stale breath tenting unwashed sheets—We abandoned you to boyhood in the body of man. Body with flaws known and not.

Body that will never explode into what its genes were ticking toward. A body with its blinds still closed, so that glow could only bar a prison.

Oh prisoner of a single bad decision, prisoner of one last irrevocable tantrum. When the body jumps the mind cannot undo. And so

because no one simply says don't die, you do.

Because You'll Die

is the one thing I can't bring myself to say when she asks why
she can't fly out the window. To her, it is a mime-
drawn portal, a rain-smudged shimmer.

I say *because you'll fall,* but she doesn't understand
the emergency in my voice, a siren-fit I pitch
to show this is serious. Sometimes

everywhere I look is gaping windows, the tipped chair,
the broken swing. Somewhere between the 30th floor and safe
the ground appears to catch us. So many moments

tense with the buried things of fate, the spring-box
of the unchangeable. I wonder how much fear
it's right to wish her, how even the truest answers I know

seem inadequate to the task of gifting her a body
that seems at times a harmony of will and water,
at times drying cement. *Because you'll get hurt,*

I say. And you will. And flesh will stubborn
into faith. This skin that scabs and scars, stories
smoothed of wounds, these brilliant breakable bones

yearning glacially toward mending. It's just part of being
both fool and soft tissue. Her existence tugs the slip-
knot of whatever wonder squeezes my heart—sunlight

snarled in a curl, bread on the hearth of morning,
clay fired to purpose in earth's oldest cradle.
Those crustaceous stars, their brittle shells of light.

At the War Remnants Museum, Formerly the Museum of American War Crimes: Agent Orange Exhibit

After the war vanished from the streets
it smoldered on in gibberish

of cells, in womb-spun flesh howled
into the trauma of living with what is

missing. A mother lifts an infant to the lens,
silently shows me what is missing

from his body, as if that's all there is
to say. And it is. In every frame,

a being formed in a new way.
Such variety, it's almost miraculous.

How stubborn, yet fragile
life is, a flame our hipbones cup

like palms. I've told myself there is no stoop
on which I would have abandoned you,

my twelve-week candle, no manger
flanked by sentinels of moonlight.

Now I wonder what your early exit
might have spared us. Should I thank

the evolutionary grace that made
my choice for me? Saigon keeps growing

away from the dead, from the past
that shimmers in the dust of the metropolis

cranes are tearing out of air.
But memory knits a kind of phosphorescence

in the genes. Yesterday, in a park
where tiny birds sing in cages

shaped like bells, a boy with a beautiful smile
and no lower half, flourished

an improvised genuflection
as I passed, his whole

body balanced on a single calloused palm.
And Saigon rises, hell-bent and ticking,

bulldozers perpetually digging
toward the ghost-itch

of a war that goes on
where we can't end it.

Not Trying

Above the city in our drawer of air
cooled enough to goose our flesh,
the fine hairs on my thighs rise

to meet yours. It is my body saying yes
to the condom, again, which is also
my body saying no.

I try not to ask myself if I answer
Chance or Fate. It makes no difference
whether or not the future is written

if I have no light to read it. But I do feel
an Icarus or Eve, one of those who fooled
with some primordial book

of matches, something I can understand
a god forbidding. Once I was your girl
lifting her hips so you could slide

off her lace panties. I can't wear that
body now, though when we giggle
over ridges made for pleasure I can feel

its island breeze, its hammock sway.
But I can't unbody what I've held
and lost, can't hull my hips

into another cradle knowing
what we flint is so dependent
on a wind we can't predict.

Knowing both how a spark can fail
and how a spark can flare.
How flame tantrums

into treetops, torching the entire
Eden where we were naked once,
and ludicrously brave.

Elegy Tangled with Silk and Spice

Evening, slick-tongued, ties up the night like a cherry stem, promise
of rain shuddering a few aimless stars. The moon gilds into a relic

of older nights, opulent with throne and spice, gutter-scents enslaved
in aristocratic kitchens. An ancient pungence leaches longing

from new mouths. These are the alleys where men pay for touch.
Too measured to call it pleasure, that methodical stoking of skin

into its own cold smolder. A bill slides across a lacquered table
and a girl drops the silk of herself to the knees of yet another

expat king. In another city I once took a job as a bar masseuse,
so I too have taken payment for my hands, stroked CEO's

and brokers into those most intimate sounds a body makes
when the mind tunes out. I've been that girl lighting the night

with the lamp of her throat, a glow that says
what you want I can give you and why is it a trick

that there's a cost? Both a little lost, Gypsy and I traipsed
Kensington's crown of fashionable bars, rubbing the shoulders

of London's workhard/playhard crowd in the popsicle glow
of glass-blown cocktails. We were taught the language of refusal

comes more naturally than yes, so we pressed our hips a bit
against their backs when we promised to relieve their stress.

I remember the night Gypsy puked all over an Italian suit,
confessed she was pregnant and wouldn't keep it. Trellis-frail,

her dress seemed afraid to touch her skin. She curled into a booth
to rest and I kept massaging necks. I always got the biggest tips

when I squeezed that chaste stalk of flesh so gentle it began to feel
like loneliness. Beyond Dong Khoi, far below the storied rooftop

bars of the Carravelle, the Continental, from every doorway
someone casts a line old as trade. Don't we all call out constantly

from the porch of ourselves? I've crammed in a subway car,
breasts silently filling with milk. I've held a man I had no plans

to love, a single egg hovering inside me, calling in the only way it can,
animal musk snared in my hair, blood blushed close as possible to where

I ended and he began. Waiting. Exposed. The night Gypsy didn't show
I worked alone, pretending I was glad I didn't have to compete for tips.

It was only later, when our boss called to say she'd hung herself from
a tree in Hampstead Heath, that I remembered finding her in the alley

outside the bar. She was smashing french-fries into a smear of ketchup
like snuffing out cigarette after cigarette. There was something dead

about her then, but I was screaming too loudly to hear her.

Unknown Soldiers

When the moon gapes between skyscrapers
like an exposed throat, I almost know

how the unbearable plateaus in the long
slit of night's half-shut eye.

I was born in a big country. I take
for granted the space

to grieve little things. And I keep
voicing this unknown chorus.

Such tiny soldiers, such unison
as they whir-whisper a fight

or flight aortal aria—*My brothers
will you die for me? Sisters, I've killed*

*for me, can't still my muscle memory
of that.* My country strikes

and strikes the match and villages disperse
as ash. Where they land, they winter.

Because I am a mother I would kill
or die for, and I can never hold the living

hard enough. Because there is so much space
between each thing I've lost,

I feel compelled to quantify each one
as less than in most any equation.

I've held a heart in me so fiercely,
but couldn't feel it

stop. Grief is a big country
with too many songs.

Voice-over, earth-pit with bones
in your mouth, spit me out.

And still this tongue
that tastes everything.

Getting There

Evening is a disaster
        of shadows.

A shadow crane falls
        across a shadow play

        ground. Night pools into open
graves below apartment blocks.

I am stagnant in this city
        that is growing all around me.
Even now
        two cranes exact
their slow ballet
        outside my window.

        I can't hear the music

that aches their impossibly extended limbs
        into wider and wider pirouette, but I see

        the wall they conjure
like a rabbit from a hat.

From my perch on the thirtieth floor
        the river seems an extension

cord carelessly dropped,
        its currents invisible
        beneath rubbery sheen.

I count twelve scaffold skyscrapers.

They possess a straight-backed grace.

Surely some music must rise through
        the straw of the magician's spine, erupting brain-
bound into the verb *to lengthen*.

A music mostly breath,
        like a yoga instructor's
                command—*extend extend*—as bodies stretch

into bridges, trees, arrows.
        The music of reaching
for its own sake,
        toward nothing but beyond.

In warrior pose,
        eyes closed, I am elastine,
orbital. I swear I feel gain,
        inch by glorious inch,

but when I open my eyes I am just the usual

limit of myself.
        Everyday another floor

        skyward. Surely the music of growth
should hurt different

from the music of destruction.
        I close my eyes, lean

        into want
                too inherent to speak.

The only name
        I know to give it:
other than.

Overdue Elegies

Elegy: Ensemble Cast

Because we are a disharmonious chorus
of breathing, cut us into paper-dolls, joined
at the palms by one of those threadbare songs
that lend a grudging tenderness to the requisite
montage. Cut to an aerial view of a city
that's always New York, even when it's made-up.
When the same night seals many windows,
let the song yawn wide as a ghost kept too long
in the skull. Cut to the terminal man, the prodigal
son. Cut to the surgeon-god who finally couldn't
save someone. Cut to the woman in labor.
Cut her perineum, cut the cord. Let the girl cut teeth
and let her use them. Let song arch into scream.
Cut to the payphone, the runaway holding her breath
while her mother calls *Hello? Hello?* Let bridge treble
dial tone. Cut to the train station, the airport,
to any place where someone is leaving because
they don't know what we do, that they are loved,
oh how they are loved. Cut to the one who is getting out
of the traffic-locked taxi to run. Let the song be large
enough to hold the ways we die together. Cut to turbulence,
oxygen masks dropping like spiders in a haunted house.
Cut to the ash world we shake from this one
with our bombings. Cut to the unimaginable
multitudes of earth calling the oldest names of god
as meteor becomes greater than moon. Let it be near
enough to shroud the ways we die alone. Cut it frame
by frame and still there is no record of what escapes.
Cut to the moment we wake to what we've lost
and the next ones where we shower and breakfast
and dress. Cut to the universe of this screen
where *pixel* translates to *star* in language only
fraction can speak. Cut one life into a mosaic
of radiant scenes. Keep cutting
until everything bleeds.

Elegy for My Brother's Childhood Monster

He still can't name it and I've no lamp
to amp the shadows into tigers

we can tame. He must be so small
inside his body now. His legs

shoot from the bed into the blankest air
where no length of his woman

warms him. I think of those big-soled feet
sometimes, just hanging there

like twin planets too large to mistake
for stars. I think of losing: relatives, teeth,

moles, the bits that compose the old
and moth-rid places where our stories

overlap. Sometimes I want to get in
the car with his childhood,

the one that looks like mine
but isn't. I want to drive with it

to some nebulous middle
state where corn is engineered

to survive just another one of many
things that must be survived.

It stands up straight in the sun,
blonde as his child-fine hair on mornings

when I woke to find him shipwrecked
in my bed. And I never asked what he ran from

in whatever wilderness he conjured
of his room. And then we grew too big

for those sweet and shapeless fears.
His hair darkened, hardened close

to his skull, the door
between us closed.

Elegy with Just Two Seasons

1

In the city where we met, we go on
        walking, hands in each other's pockets, seeking
any shadowed space
        large enough to hold two bodies, leaning.

We were students, we had no money, or just enough
        to split a pint and pack of cigarettes. Do you recall,
my love, how we kept falling
        off your single bed? So we lay your mattress on the floor
    beneath a window open to each passing gull's bright cry.

For awhile it was summer and the nights were almost warm.

2

            It was winter
    and the pill you slipped beneath my tongue made me molten,
            long-limbed, lazy and J. kept talking
        about Jesus, saying *what have I accomplished* and I was thinking how
I didn't have to look so high

            to make myself feel low.
                It was winter and we should have realized
    when he was laying out his crimes he was saying
        his goodbye. And I remembered how you'd warned me
J. can get a little dark sometimes.

3

I remember frost
        on iron railings, rust wrought into shards
            by salt and time,

how they bit into my palms when he vanished
        from the ledge, a Cheshire cat,
            leaving only his unreadable grin behind.

4

It was winter. It was one week into a new year and I held
the clothes his girlfriend chose on my lap inside a plastic
      bag. The train was cold inside and cut
across the ice-spiked fields of Sussex and I hoped we'd never reach
      the mortuary. Later, you stepped into my shower and I was afraid

           of your desire,
     and of mine and I couldn't meet his girlfriend's eye
outside the crematorium when you sought between my glove and sleeve
     a slim sliver of wrist. Aren't we lucky, darling?

We outlived them all. Crashed through all those young loves
        tucked into the pub's dark corners, our bodies fused
          into a wrecking ball.

5

It was winter. It was near dark in the city
     where we met. It was winter. It was Boxing Day,
my love, and we'd stayed in bed so late
        the sun had nearly set. We walked along the seawall,
you rolled a joint you called a spliff and we passed it back and forth
     with our gloved fingers. Remember that rec center
        across from Palace Pier? The steamed-up basement windows?

We heard children laughing and I removed my glove to clear the glass.
They were splashing. They were diving. They were hurtling headfirst,

     flying, down plastic waterslides
        inside a world of green. It was winter
in a city with a heart that beat like summer
and there was your hand over mine,
    a sense of possibility,
       and the scent of chlorine.

Not Her Elegy

Her words cast a chill
glow on the side of the road
a long time ago. Her first husband

is drunk, slumped in the passenger seat,
and she's driving too slow,
the headlights swamped

by tule fog. A girl hovers
on the gravel shoulder.
Ghost. Not thought, but known

and also *I can't have a child
with this man.* And I shiver.
In another story, she runs

a fire road at dusk. The forest dims.
Redwoods lacquer into arrows.
Tiny gray moths smoke slashes

of light. *Air so thick I couldn't run
through it.* My own body charges
with knowing the end already

because I've heard it so many times.
By morning, another woman's body
darkens moss beside the stream.

Sometimes when I pass that bend
in the road, I blind my periphery.
Others I slow, rubber-necking

for ghosts. Today I sip coffee
in the house I grew in, skim
the story of a woman in Lahore

on her way to court to ask for
a divorce. Witnesses say a car
slowed, the window unrolled

and I feel the cold flash
between me and the word
stoned. Outside she shrieks

on the hose, shatters bees from
rhododendrons and I remember
the way she casually untied the knot

at the base of her skull while she spoke,
how when her hair leapt to her shoulders
it seemed the very definition of grace.

Elegy, March 11th 2011

"The March 11, magnitude 9.0 earthquake in Japan may have
shortened the length of each Earth day and shifted its axis.
But don't worry—you won't notice the difference."

—Nasa.gov article

The night you died the earth shifted
6.5 inches on its axis. 1.8 microseconds

subtracted from our days. Such changes
cannot be registered in artificial light.

The paper gown shelled your chest
like a knight's breast plate, invisible

helmet lifted to reveal the shorn head
of a martyred saint. On our side of the world

it was the dark side of morning.
Japan could not be reached

for comment. Listen: there is loss
and then the landscape

of its wake. We've been living
here for years. We skip over

absence like a groove in a well-
loved song, a blink-size space

that holds all the things you'll never say.
Your friends keep getting married,

having babies, your husband falls
in and out of grace, and that book you loved

was made into a movie. Some missing
become survivors, some are never

found. Most are what's expected,
buried. We commemorate

the shaking, the flood, the flat-line.
There are always dates to ache between.

Now the cherry tree outside
your bedroom window is losing

its leaves again. You didn't feel
your heels stick to the smashed fruit

on the patio, didn't smell the blossoms,
pink in the blonde sun. You didn't see

your husband's face when the alarm
you'd set woke him from his shell-

shocked sleep the morning after
the night you died. The way

those bald branches spread—
shatter lines in the porcelain sky.

Elegy with Scrambled Itinerary

2 to 3 months prior to death:

Hospice nurses seem too practical to be angels, but news they do deliver. For example: A pamphlet on the nightstand reveals the soul leaves the body in stages, like grief. I'm still deciding what I believe absent in the recently deceased. But some disgruntled tenant paces the condemned structure that was my grandmother.

86 years prior to death:

A girl in a tarnished mirror decides she doesn't like her ears.

2 to 3 Weeks Prior to Death:

We begin to trash what's left before the earth can repossess. Her fingers pry callouses like floorboards from her palms. Teeth steadily strip layer after layer of skin from her lip. The single muscle of her dying thrashes clear of sheets and hands and jellied blobs that promise weak-tea sustenance.

4-5 years prior to death:

Don't grow old, she says.

Unknowable years prior to death:

I play runaway beneath a lilac bush. I can still be nothing until someone calls my name.

Unknowable days prior to death:

All children are lonely in this way. Strangers enter the room, hold fingers to her wrist, her neck. When they leave I hold my ear to her chest. She answers like a seashell. I remember the lilac bush, bees ballooning its scent and I held the string, no longer a girl, but a kind of lifting.

28,530 days prior to death:

Light falls like an ax through the glades. She sees the moment of her leaving racing toward her through the firebrand autumn trees.

4-5 weeks prior to death:

Something must be terribly wrong with me, she says, *it seems like I'm alone so much of the time.* Yes, childhood seems a fitting bookend.

2 to 3 minutes prior to death:

There is so much space between each breath it's impossible to mark the moment of transition, when the body at last shudders out whatever it has to.

2 to 3 days prior to death:

She screams *There are worms!* We tell her they're caterpillars. She screams *There are caterpillars!* When the mind is beyond association it doesn't matter who feasts on what remains.

3 to 4 months prior to death:

Childhood mostly remains. Hayfever, coaldust, a constant cough in rural West Virginia, a town with two churches and nothing better to do than confess at both on Sundays.

2 to 3 days prior to death:

They seem too practical to be angels, but mercy they deliver in little yellow vials. Beneath the lid of her sleep she says goodbye to all of her ages.

1 to 2 days prior to death:

Even morphine cannot make her sleep.

1 week prior to death:

I contemplate wrapping her like an infant, a drive to the coast through silence that rings a seashell's undertow tongue. I can almost see the blown bodies of cows hovering in pastures sick with green. Eyes so large tiny insects oar their glaze.

5 days prior to death:

It is too late for world in a windshield. A test: Look Grandma, the ocean. *Oh yes,* she murmurs through closed eyes, *oh yes.*

Elegy for a Sea Hare

It's the size of my thigh, pockmarked
as an overripe papaya, and exudes
a similar oozy heaviness. An older boy

prods it with a stick and the creature opens
some hidden fount of strangeness, inking
purple into the yipping wavelets. *What is it?*

whispers a woman who isn't from here. I tell her
I've never seen one before in my life, though
I learned to swim in this bay, shaped kingdoms

of this same motley sand. My parents own
a double plot a mile south, have planted yellow roses
whose roots they'll feed. I've already uprooted myself

so many times, as if no soil can hold me,
but it will hold me. Someone breathes
I think its dying. And it is. Gently, quietly,

nameless beneath our curious eyes. What guides
us toward the us-shaped space we die in?
My grandmother, born in coal-country West Virginia,

rode her children's wake all the way to California,
only to die within a handful of childhood memories
scored so deep into her being they couldn't be erased

by her disease. Stranger, with your mucous-sheen,
your leprous peelings, who would touch you?
Stranger, you reek of coral reefs, aquamarines and neons

lit with lethal nectars. Not this snake-tongue bay,
flicking out, flicking in, between blonde pasture manged
by cattle. Still, these mudflat tides, they lift you,

lull you into whatever is your version of being
a body aliened by landscape, an itinerary
of indecipherable scars. I've never wanted to die

beside this bay, so why not let these tides be
trade winds. Let me wash up in the tropics whence
you, Stranger, came. Somewhere fragrant with night-

crushed jasmine and kaleidoscopic rot. Let me be
ship-wrecked by some fever to which the natives have
been long immune. Let them guess. They'll never guess

I'm flat on my back on that old raft, crumbling
a piece of salt-cured kelp between my fingers,
watching the eternal coastal fog crest the ridge,

engulf me like a tsunami.

And Away

If No Energy Can Be Created or Destroyed

Before she turned the ultrasound
away, I saw my tiny unmanned satellite.

And distance. Unbridgeable.
I trusted that wand to illuminate

like a flashlight my own dear
and darkly growing, but I saw only

moonscape, basalt
without a fleck of pyrite.

Foolish to wish
and faith at the same time.

There's no pulse
to you, moon, no sea

foam from which to pearl a mortal
breath, no fins to foot

or follow. Inside, I maintain
my chronic summer, roughly

37 trillion cells, each so unknown,
it might as well be that lonely edge

where orbits slow and bodies drift
helplessly apart.

With such gravity we hold you,
moon. With such ease

you tug us into arms and swords
to fall on. A woman I don't know

wrote *I feel like a walking tomb.*
I'm still trying to name the way.

Perhaps this—the indistinguishable dark
where the moon still is, but has turned

its face from us.

After Dark

The skyscraper beside this skyscraper
is knee-high, but each week adds
another floor, shaves another arc

from the sphere my belly should have waxed.
At night I feel the city growing, a jackhammer
in my torso like second heart, metal kicked

into the gong of alignment. It's like we're living
in one giant open-air mine, our breach exploding
solid sky. And the shattering is a million

motorbikes schooling alleys too narrow
to map. The shattering is a mosaic of skyline
sequinning the river's black sash.

It shimmers in the mosquito dusk and gathers
in tangles of sewage and lotus, in new slums
where old plagues still sheen in the gutters.

Even through blackout blinds all that light
keeps seeping in like water, so I keep
dreaming night back into my body,

that yearned for fern-tinged dark of any
half-baked edenscape. And before it was
a garden it was a wilderness and until

it is a garden it cannot be a farm, cannot feed
the open mouths of all these skyscraped windows.
Once this was a village. Once this was a war.

Once this was a city abandoned to its falling
ever upward into this startling clear—tomorrow
is a box we trace in air, then try to live in.

Getting Around: By Taxi

How many lives tremble at this single stoplight? So many
profiles fastened on the place where they are going.

From inside the air-conditioned cab, I play at catching eyes,
      throw them back. I keep thinking of that damn REM video,

      where everyone gets out of their cars. As if it's that easy
to step out of place. Sometimes I get lost in my own

the way I get lost in this city. On every moped a little room
      is balanced. A woman unclips her helmet so her lover can hood

      her hair from the rain. A woman unbuttons her blouse
to nurse a swaddled infant. Siblings, sardined between

their parents, squabble sleepily. So many intimacies,
      so little immediacy. Every morning, thirty-stories

      up, I treadmill my body weapon-ready. My conditions
are that this city keep its goddamn hands to itself.

      My conditions go against my wishes. A wavering
what-if in the glass where my cheek rests

mouths one of the old names I crave (hint, it isn't wife
      or mother). True, sometimes I sing my darlings to sleep

      just so I can slip away, but I'll never be insane enough
to walk toward the woman I never was,

      the one who lives only in the eyes of men
            I'll never touch. At intersections, we come to

like sleepers yanked from dreams by the invisible leash
      of need, thirst or just the daily surrender to the light

that tells us when to stay.

Because It's Been Too Long Since I Wrote a Love Poem

There was one tenet of my faith: Between us we could carry
everything we'd need. In airports, train stations, terminals
of every sort, we connected dots on maps into a rosary.
Oh holy names, oh hallowed strings of foreign sounds.
Those fervent backstreets, old quarters labyrinthine
as the empires that shaped them, night markets powered by
drooping cables, thick and tangled as jungle vines. Piazzas, zocalos,
plazas clad in cobblestone. My God cobblestones! If only every city
could be cobbled, lantern-lit and rain-lacquered, red-roofed and slanted.
If only every house could be white-washed adobe or ramshackle
colonial mansion. I swear my bones have crackled with joy
at begonias blaring like megaphones from balconies. To stumble upon
a little fountain feathered with algae, a mural like a misplaced sunset
smeared across an abandoned shopfront. How are we born knowing
to find beauty in the relics we have made, remade, preserved
and warred for? We napped in hammocks rocked by desert breeze,
wafted fever-winds choppered in from some bonfire of fragrant trees.
How heat drugs to opium in the lungs. How we ran from storms
that ended as soon as we found shelter. How we sheltered in hostels,
cabanas, tents and all-night buses. Our aura of sunscreen, sweat
and deet. How mosquito net and headlamp shrouded any sagging cot
in votive light. You were my accomplice runaway, my willingly,
carrier of extra weight, keeper of the moneybelt and passports
so I could drift in peasant skirts, my shared meal, my soon-to-be,
my lost and here and hopelessly. Amid all the ten-years-too-lates,
the overpriced-once-greats, we found that pristine palm-lined beach,
that perfectly spiced plate, that shrine twined with banyan tree.
We lived it and we left, lived and left, and left again. It was you
and me, it was ours. It was years before I missed anything.

Time Zones at a Glance

Each day much the same
and unrepeatable. The sunset

sudden and too
brief, and the afterward

is always the longest
evening. When there's nothing left

to do with the day, the playground fills
with sweaty palms and hairlines,

with little hot-potato bodies, intolerable
to hold. And half a chalk-drawn moon,

a single powdered cheek
the dark will soon slap

into a ringing glow.
Tossled palms

against a bleached-out sky and I
can almost feel the curvature of earth,

the tilting of the place I am
into the place I've been.

Round and round, the tilting
of today into tonight into yesterday.

I'm thinking of all
the people who once shared

the same sorry plot of space
and time, now sticking out like pins

on a map of cities
I'll never visit.

Though tonight I want to
sit on all their couches,

bounce their babies on my knee.
Dusk and I'm still a fool

for that last light, the way it turns
everything to bone

and yearning. I'm a sucker
in the most old-fashioned way.

Dusk tells me beauty is enough
and every time I buy it.

As a girl I watched sunsets
on the shed roof,

a private beach of shingle and shale,
a dark-lapped raft

I dreamed on.
Is there anything more lonely

than a grieving no one shares?
Singular and lovely

like the moon is, alone up there
amongst all those frost-tipped stars.

There are thoughts I keep for no reason
other than I trust no way to speak them.

Tonight I swear I'd try.
The earth spins, spins me,

but things stay much the same
distance apart.

At the War Remnant's Museum, formerly the Museum of American War Crimes: Reporters Exhibit

This is the storyboard of how
our consciousness
passed over Vietnam
like an ultrasound.

> In a dated den
> in a Chicago suburb
> my teenage mother sounds
> out the name of a country

she's never heard of.
Her parent's black and white
TV blares an indiscriminate blur
of handshaking diplomats,

> foliage and conical hats,
> a human mass, faceless,
> merged. My mother doesn't
> see her war, not yet.

But the name is seed
enough to root in her.
Decades later she will tour
the Cu Chi Tunnels, the DMZ.

> Decades sooner, the boys
> she knows start leaving.
> Black and white armies
> mutate dark and light

across America's screens
as if there's only one weak-eyed
camera to pan the scene. Gradually
Vietnam comes into focus. Technicolor.

Undeniable. Impossible,
how all that black brims
to blood. For a while
she believes folksongs

and weed can supple
bayonets into reeds. In smoke-
filled offices in Boston, she counsels
draft-age boys to flee. We divide

        into those who serve and those
        who serve another purpose. Iconic
        images flood in, that girl running
        from her own burning skin,

that nun falling to flame.
Faces flashed into the many
gargoyles of suffering.
A show, we can't stop

        watching. Decades later, during
        the televised inception of another
        war, my mother sees fireflies
        above her Midwest lawn

but the anchor assures her
these are bombs, hovering
over Baghdad. Cable whispers
Listen! War is always there

        the way our own heartbeat is
        whenever we tune in.
        Decades earlier, my mother
        learns to say *Not in our name.*

We mispronounce the names
of the cities we are bombing.
America grows a franken-nation
in the belly of our rabbit ear TVs.

Memorial Day, decades later
and my mother salutes a regiment
of graves, sharp-white as baby teeth.
A trumpet sounds as if to shake them

from the gum of our green lawns.
In Saigon, there is no war outside,
only the after. And the after
is a construction site.

But at night, the girl in the picture runs
toward us. So clear in her agony
we have to look away
before she can be born.

Elegy with Due Date

The river is not a road so is an invitation
for the mind to roam the spaces between

cities where mines still pine like bulbs
for a springtime-worth of weight.

Don't all seeds long to blossom
their coiled code? Even the dead

don't know how to stay
closed, worming as they do, rooting

as they do. Leafing new
into the same sweet light.

The river reveals nothing
of where things vanish to,

only the ghost-pool
of my own gaze.

This date knives
right through, passes

like any other day. My body changes,
but less vividly. I can only call it healing.

I can only heal, as the battlefields
this river feeds do, scabbing green

over the soldier graves, the child graves,
there is nothing it can't stomach

into fuel. It should be easy to stomach
loss the size of a walnut,

an apricot, when there are more atoms
in my body than stars

in the known universe. Tell me
creation pearled blindly into us

so it could know itself. I don't know
if we are the reflection

or if God refracts nightly into stars
to shame us. Either way, we're mostly space

and survival. We can only stay dead
a little while, before green muscles in

to wake us.

In Context: Mekong Delta

Somewhere, in a place entirely unlike
this one, the crown of the Mekong fissures
Earth's tallest granite, thrust skyward

by the collision of continents that might
as well be gods in a myth we made,
so we could nod, say *ah* this is how

this came to be. The Mekong does not
know it is destined to lose itself
in the South China Sea, does not know

it is a river. For now it is only a melting
out of silence, a shifting from static
into motion. In the Himalayas

streams blossom with the trees,
glitter their own little Shangri-las
from every cliff and crag and crevice,

until the season avalanches into a tumult
of rapids, ripping new canyons through hills
that only look like they are standing still.

Land of a million elephants, land of smiles,
kingdoms, pagodas, wars working their way
through the salt mines of unwon minds.

When foothills spill into killing fields,
the Mekong yawns wide enough to live
on, to buy and sell on. To be sold on.

Whatever language it has gathered in its rushing
over stones, under bridges, in its lugging
of the dropped, the drowned, the used,

it will lose. Every second it is different
water whispering *never again never
again.* If we could ride it like a many-headed

serpent as it splays into the sea, for a while
it would remain its own current. But eventually
whatever body it's become in its loose holding,

whatever sound it has become in its one yearning
toward exactly this disappearing, is replaced
by whatever the sea says when it forgets

the chant it repeats on every beach,
the one we mistranslate *ash to ash,
dust to dust.*

Trying

River palms clasp muscular to a slip-bank starred with the spectrum
of shattered glass—amber, emerald, bluebottle—and dragonflies

sip river, sip rain. In the lowlands the river is morning-slow and body-
warm, no rush in it, only a perpetual opening into larger

and larger dreams. The palm trees sway like cobras. Their endless
necks explode into the bedhead havoc of frazzled fronds, and banana leaf

shadows snap open like fans. I am in the chartless part of waiting, no form
of divination I can trust. My own intuition, a demagnetized compass,

spinning with every brush of heat-stoked wind. So the earth hula-hoops
our weather in the name of balance, warm sinks to cool, hot and cold

crash into rain, thrill into lightning. Into warning. This world
and the windows where we watch it from, the many faiths we peer from,

can't be trusted. Still, this humming of a sweet what-if. Tiny birds
I haven't learned the names of, or how to spell their songs.

The garden heavy with frogs. Even their leaps seem weighted,
unlike the birds and dragonflies, which seem less like bodies and more

like snarls of air. And I can't stop staring at water—sea river rain—
hypnotic we call it, whatever breaks the trance of ourselves.

Trying

The moon fat and golden as the belly I touched
today in a pagoda full of other bellies, and now
the sea curls in like a cat with stars in its fur,
nuzzles the dust from my feet, finds every crease
where the heat-sick day still clings,
                                        and because
there is no prayer small enough to keep inside me
I say aloud *I want to start new,* and though there is
only sea here, sea and that plump summer moon
laying out its pier of light, whatever remains of the night
rings with hearing,
                        and then there is your body
as it's always been, above me, the sand cupping me
like water, sand still the ghost of itself, and morning
a promise on the ridge of your nose, the plain
of your cheeks,
                    and the body
cannot fail to be a landscape, with its weird weather
and predictable tides, and I am leaning out
from mine again, a small way into yours,
                                            and inside
the pagoda I chose one belly for its shine, and now
I say the moon is full, meaning it is still half dark,
and that tiny question mark hooks once again
into the deepest yes of my flesh.

Beach Days

I think we love the beach because we can all crawl out of the sea again,
lizard the sand like some Gallapagos scene. But I love the beach most
when I leave it, when I wash it from my skin under a cool shower,
walk around the hotel room naked, lie down on the fresh-made bed
naked, and sleep in the same sea I spent all morning fighting.

Our daughter sleeps through the day's fevered center and outside
goes on blossoming its smoke and songs without us, blissfully
without us. We have learned our waiting here. We wait as humans
have always waited, on shores and mountains, for the sun to set,
watching for the moment beauty lessens so we can turn away from it.

I remake the beauty of each day in sleep's choreography. In the backyard
drive-in of the behind part of my looking. Body lifting with remembered
waves, or swaying with winding roads, mountains snared in a vision
stowed away, unnoticed, until the body rests in a dark I've built for it,
a dark grace built for it, of blinds and lids and a deeper place to fall.

According to the theory of infinite halfway points, there is a space
between us we can never cross, and there was something urgent
that I meant to tell you. But the mind wanders. Hands and toes
and tongues wander too. Listen: the white-noise

of cicadas has a rising to it, a loudness capable of launching
the little rocket of a self. Or even this village, light as it is
with bamboo walls and palm-frond roofs. It trembles
as if it could blow away or stay a thousand years.

Bamboo leaves flick little fish of bright into the shadow-spell
we've cast and possible fades to impossible the way the sun disappears
long before its light. And we, distracted by the smokescreen carnival
of color left behind, don't notice that everywhere behind us
it is already night.

Trying

In this festival of tourists we are ready to celebrate
anything—a paper boat clutching a single candle,

the river fluttering back the colored lights
we lend it. Autumnal forest-fire of abandoned

leaves. Each red and orange offering blooms
the darkness deeper in between. A darkness

muscular as lips chanting in a language of echo
and taboo. It snakes a dance

into my deepest suppleness, the changeable neon
of flesh molten with ancient sin. How my spine

wants to willow to that golden calf, how my forehead
wants to feel the give of pagan earth. Let's pretend

frangipani is the fragrance of stars. Let's scar these
ancestral rites with our fresh flames. Pleas

new only in how whimsically they are whispered
in the heart. The way a child blows out every candle

on her cake, her wish half-formed, a shapeless wanting.
The vaguest itch that smarts to sharp of prayer

only when it goes ungranted.

And Away

In this space we steeple of our bones, in that hollow,
I hide my other cheek, the one I refuse
the hand of God. I know, I know—

we do what we must. Weave a bassinet of water
hyacinth, ignore the newborn latch of mud
to toes. Let go, let go. What the current doesn't claim,

the dirt will. The unborn must still be birthed,
that is the body's truth. Some things must enter
the world unfinished, a graft of clot and ghost.

A haunting houred in winter. I watched light lengthen
as the bleeding dimmed. Ended enough to miss it.
I've never been good enough at holding on

to pain. The body's truth: nausea stagnates
into an ugly hunger. Winter ends and I blue
print dreams in which I find you inside mustard jars,

squash blossoms, tins of semolina, but sleep's
architects sift moths of the flour of your flesh.
Summer now and still the river.

And when I lay you down in your bed of reeds,
it is not a choice, but a season. If we must fall
to arrive then we must leave by rising.

I gather more and more view into my gaze.
The city of lost-and-found teeters on
where-do-we-go-from-here, a shrapnel gleam

in the immensity of this green, this country that remains
an opacity. But something of it scars my eye, so long
and lonely in its looking, and whatever I carry

out of here feels grave-robbed, though I know
it is the most elemental conjuring of this body
that only wants to last.

Acknowledgments

Thank you to the editors of the following journals in which some of these poems first appeared:

Connotation Press: An Online Artifact: "Elegy Proving Airplanes Don't Fly on Shared Belief," "Elegy for My Brother's Childhood Monster," "Elegy with Scrambled Itinerary," and "Elegy for a Sea Hare"

Hermeneutic Chaos: "In Context: This Latitude of Air" and "Unknown Soldiers"

Matter: "At the War Remnants Museum, formerly the Museum of American War Crimes: Unknown Soldier" and "At the War Remnants Museum, formerly the Museum of American War Crimes: Agent Orange Exhibit"

The Pinch Literary Journal: "If No Energy Can Be Created Or Destroyed"

Tinderbox Poetry Journal: "Elegy Tangled with Silk and Spice" and "Elegy with Due Date"

Vinyl Poetry and Prose: "Prayer for Fertile Ground"

I want to thank Tony Barnstone and the National Federation of State Poetry Societies for selecting this book.

I will always be grateful for my SDSU MFA class of 2013 cohort, who continue to inspire me from afar with their creativity, generosity, and talent: Annette, Laura, Kaitlin, Susan, Rachel, Francine, Erica, Danielle, Seretta, Aimee, Dave, and Jen. I also want to add Crystal, Nicole, Daniela, Scott, and Garrett, who were in different classes, but continue to offer their enthusiasm and support.

I am forever indebted to the phenomenal Carly Joy Miller for tirelessly reading and commenting on nearly everything I've written and for always knowing the perfect edits to make.

A special thank you to my Mill Valley poetry group (Ella, Angelika, Miriam, Suzanne, Bruce, Edward, and Barbara), and our fearless leader, Tom Centolella, for providing feedback on many of these poems.

Thank you too, to the many teachers who have shaped my writing over the years: Sandra Alcosser, Ilya Kaminsky, Marilyn Chin, Kate Gale, Steve Kowit, Gabrielle Calvocoressi, Shadab Zeest Hashmi, Piotr Florczyk, Jenny Minniti-Shippey, Julie Bruck, and Matthew Lippman.

Thank you to the Sundress Academy of the Arts, for my residency at Firefly Farms where some of these poems were written and revised.

And always and forever my love and gratitude to my husband, daughters, parents, brother, family, and friends. You all make the poetry possible.

THE NATIONAL FEDERATION OF STATE POETRY SOCIETIES
STEVENS POETRY MANUSCRIPT COMPETITION

The National Federation of State Poetry Societies (NFSPS) is a nonprofit organization focused on poetry and education, which sponsors fifty annual poetry contests, the winners of which appear in the anthology *Encore*. NFSPS also sponsors the annual Stevens Poetry Manuscript Competition for the best collection of poems by a single poet. The contest winner receives a cash prize of $1,000, publication by NFSPS Press, and fifty copies of his or her prize-winning book. The annual deadline is October 15th, the decision is announced in January, and the prize-winning book is published in June. Complete submission guidelines are available from the NFSPS website at www.nfsps.com, where winning books and editions of *Encore* can be ordered.

PAST STEVENS POETRY MANUSCRIPT
COMPETITION WINNERS

2015
Midnight River, by Laura L. Hansen (Rochester Hills, MI: NFSPS Press, 2016). Judge: Bruce Dethlefsen.

2014
Beast, by Mara Adamitz Scrupe (Rochester Hills, MI: NFSPS Press, 2015). Judge: John Witte.

2013
Breaking Weather, by Betsy Hughes (Rochester Hills, MI: NFSPS Press, 2014). Judge: Glenna Holloway.

2012
Full Cry, by Lisa Ampleman (Rochester Hills, MI: NFSPS Press, 2013). Judge: Maggie Anderson.

2011
Good Reason, by Jennifer Habel (Rochester Hills, MI: NFSPS Press, 2012). Judge: Jessica Garratt.

2010
Lines from the Surgeon's Children, 1862-1865, by Rawdon Tomlinson (Rochester Hills, MI: NFSPS Press, 2011). Judge: Lola Haskins.

2009
Come In, We're Open, by Sara Ries (Rochester Hills, MI: NFSPS Press, 2010). Judge: Ralph Burns.

2008
Bear Country, by Dana Sonnenschein (Rochester Hills, MI: NFSPS Press, 2009). Judge: Carolyne Wright.

2007
Capturing the Dead, by Daniel Nathan Terry (Rochester Hills, MI: NFSPS Press, 2008). Judge: Jeff Gundy.

2006
The Meager Life and Modest Times of Pop Thorndale, by W. T. Pfefferle (Rochester Hills, MI: NFSPS Press, 2007). Judge: Patricia Fargnoli.

2005

Harvest, by Budd Powell Mahan (Rochester Hills, MI: NFSPS Press, 2006). Judge: Lawson Inada.

2004

Aqua Curves, by Karen Braucher (Rochester Hills, MI: NFSPS Press, 2005). Judge: Peter Meinke.

2003

The Zen Piano Mover, by Jeanne Wagner (Rochester Hills, MI: NFSPS Press, 2004). Judge: Ruth Berman.

2002

A Thousand Bonds: Marie Curie and the Discovery of Radium, by Eleanor Swanson (Rochester Hills, MI: NFSPS Press, 2003). Judge: Bruce Eastman.

2001

The Fine Art of Postponement, by Jane Bailey (Rochester Hills, MI: NFSPS Press, 2002). Judge: Donna Salli.

2000

The Stones for a Pillow, by Diane Glancy (Rochester Hills, MI: NFSPS Press, 2001). Judge: David Sutherland.

1999

Binoculars, by Douglas Lawder (Rochester Hills, MI: NFSPS Press, 2000). Judge: Kenneth Brewer.

1998

Singing in the Key of L, by Barbara Nightingale (Rochester Hills, MI: NFSPS Press, 1999). Judge: Sue Brannan Walker.

1997

Weighed in the Balances, by Alan Birkelbach (Austin, TX: Plainview Press, 1998). Judge: Anne Marx.

1996

Shadowless Flight, by Todd Palmer (Deerfield, IL: Lake Shore Publishing, 1997). Judge: Michael Bugeja.

1995

I Have Learned Five Things, by Elaine Christensen (Deerfield, IL: Lake Shore Publishing, 1996). Judge: Michael Dennis Browne.

1994

A Common Language, by Kathryn Clement (Deerfield, IL: Lake Shore Publishing, 1995). Judge: David Baker.

Made in the USA
Las Vegas, NV
25 February 2021

18556485R00046